Silly Jokes
for
Silly Kids

by Silly Willy

Also Available:

Question: Why did the banana go to the doctor?

Answer: Because it wasn't peeling well!

Q: What did the banana say to the elephant?

A: **Nothing. Bananas can't talk, silly!**

Q: What do you call an alligator in a vest?
A: An Investi-gator!

Q: What did the stamp say to the envelope?
A: Stick with me and we will go places!

Q: What did the pencil say to the other pencil?
A: You're looking sharp!

Q: What fruit teases you a lot?
A: A Ba na..na..na..na..na!

Q: What is as big as an elephant but weighs nothing?
A: Its shadow!

Q: Why did the picture go to jail?
A: Because it was framed!

Q: What do you call a baby monkey?
A: A chimp off the old block!

Q: What kind of bed does a mermaid sleep in?

A: **A water bed!**

Q: Who earns a living driving their customers away?

A: **A taxi driver!**

Q: Why did the computer go to the doctor?
A: **Because it had a virus!**

Q: What do you call a retired vegetable?
A: **A has-bean!**

Q: Why do fish live in salt water?
A: **Because pepper makes them sneeze!**

Q: What do you get when you cross a
snowman with a vampire?
A: **Frostbite!**

Q: Why are frogs so happy?
A: They eat whatever bugs them!

Q: What ended in 1895?
A: **1894!**

Q: What season is it when you are on a trampoline?

A: **Spring time.**

Q: What did the little mountain say to the big mountain?

A: **Hi Cliff!**

Q: What did the alien say to the garden?

A: **Take me to your weeder!**

Q: What is the difference between a school teacher and a train?

A: **The teacher says spit your gum out and the train says "chew chew chew"!**

Q: What sound do porcupines make when they kiss?

A: **Ouch!**

Q: Did you hear the joke about the roof?

A: **Never mind, it's over your head!**

Q: Why are pirates called pirates?

A: **Because they arrrrr.**

Q: What did the boy ghost say to the girl ghost?

A: **You look boo-tiful tonight!**

Q: What do prisoners use to call each other?

A: **Cell phones!**

Q: Why couldn't the pirate play cards?

A: Because he was sitting on the deck!

Q: What did one elevator say to the other elevator?

A: I think I'm coming down with something!

Q: How do you make an Octopus laugh?

A: With ten-tickles!

Q: Why can't your nose be 12 inches long?

A: Because then it would be a foot!

Q: When is it bad luck to be followed by a black cat?

A: **When you're a mouse!**

Q: What has four wheels and flies?

A: **A garbage truck!**

Q: What starts with a P, ends with an E, and has a million letters in it?

A: **Post Office!**

Q: What did the blanket say to the bed?
A: **Don't worry, I've got you covered!**

Q: Why should you take a pencil to bed?
A: **To draw the curtains!**

Q: What kind of button won't unbutton?
A: **A bellybutton!**

Q: Why did the tomato turn red?
A: **It saw the salad dressing!**

Q: What did the judge say when the skunk walked in the court room?

A: Odor in the court!

Q: Why was the Egyptian girl worried?

A: Because her Daddy was a Mummy!

Q: Why don't skeletons fight each other?
A: **They don't have the guts!**

Q: Why was the student's report card wet?
A: **It was below C level!**

Q: What did the traffic light say to the car?
A: **Don't look, I'm changing!**

Q: What streets do ghosts haunt?
A: **Dead ends!**

Q: Why did the man with one hand cross the road?
A: **To get to the second hand shop!**

Q: Why did the robber take a bath?
A: Because he wanted to make a clean getaway!

Q: What did the judge say to the dentist?
A: Do you swear to pull the tooth, the whole tooth and nothing but the tooth!

Q: Have you heard the joke about the butter?
A: I better not tell you, it might spread!

Q: Why did the boy tiptoe past the medicine cabinet?
A: He didn't want to wake the sleeping pills!

Q: Why did the cookie go to the hospital?
A: He felt crummy!

Q: When do you stop at green and go at red?
A: When you're eating a watermelon!

Q: How did the farmer mend his pants?
A: With cabbage patches!

Q: Why did the baby strawberry cry?
A: Because his parents were in a jam!

Q: Why were the teacher's eyes crossed?
A: She couldn't control her pupils!

Q: What do you call a bear with no socks on?
A: Bare-foot!

Q: What kind of shoes do all spies wear?
A: Sneakers!

Q: Why did the boy eat his homework?
A: Because his teacher said it was a piece of cake!

Q: What can you serve but never eat?
A: A tennis ball.

Q: What runs but doesn't get anywhere?
A: A refrigerator!

Q: Why is Basketball such a messy sport?
A: Because you dribble on the floor!

Q: How do you communicate with a fish?
A: Drop him a line!

Q: Where do sheep go to get haircuts?
A: To the Baa Baa shop!

Q: What does a shark like to eat with peanut butter?
A: Jellyfish!

Q: Why can a leopard not hide?
A: Because he'll always be spotted!

Q: What do you get when you cross a cat with a lemon?

A: A sour puss!

Q: Why do birds fly south for the winter?

A: It's easier than walking!

Q: How do you know that carrots are good for your eyesight?

A: Have you ever seen a rabbit wearing glasses?

I don't like my job as an origami teacher, too much paperwork.

Q: Why are some fish at the bottom of the ocean?

A: Because they dropped out of school!

Q: What happened to the wooden car with wooden wheels and a wooden engine?

A: It wooden go!

Q: When's the best time to go to the dentist?

A: Tooth-hurty!

Q: Why did the child study in the airplane?
A: **He wanted a higher education!**

Q: Why didn't the 11 year old go to the pirate movie?
A: **Because it was rated arrrrr!**

Q: What's the difference between Ms. and Mrs.?
A: **Mr.**

Q: Where does a tree store their stuff?
A: **In their trunk!**

Q: What did the nose say to the finger?
A: Stop picking on me!

Q: What did the tie say to the hat?
A: You go on ahead and I'll hang around!

Q: Why can you never trust atoms?
A: They make up everything!

Want to hear a dirty joke? A kid jumped into a mud puddle.
Want to hear a clean joke? A kid jumped into the bath.

Q: What did they say to the man who went for a job at the print shop?

A: Sorry, you're not the right type!

Q: What do fish call a submarine?

A: A can of people!

Q: What did the lettuce say to the celery?

A: Quit stalking me!

Q: Why do witches ride broomsticks?
A: Because vacuum cleaners are too heavy!

Q: Where does bad light go?
A: To prism!

Q: What is square and green?
A: A lemon in disguise!

Q: What do you call an angry pea?
A: Grump-pea!

Q: What did the fly say when it flew into a window?
A: If I had more guts I'd do that again!

I had a dream I was a muffler and I woke up exhausted.

Q: Why did the hen cross the road?
A: **To prove she wasn't chicken!**

Q: What do you call two banana peels?
A: **A pair of slippers!**

Q: What did the eye say to the other eye?
A: **Between you and me something smells!**

Q: What did the hammer say to the piece of wood?

A: We nailed it!

Q: What goes ha ha ha plonk?

A: A skeleton laughing his head off!

Q: Which vegie plays sport?

A: Squash.

Q: What is the different between a piano and
a fish?

A: You can't tuna fish!

Q: Why did the orange stop in the middle of
the road?

A: Because he ran out of juice.

Q: Why was the piano on the porch?

A: Because he forgot his keys!

Q: Why did the man get thrown out of the banana factory?

A: Because he kept throwing the bent ones away!

Q: Why is a snail the strongest animal?

A: Because it can carry its house on its back!

Q: What do you call a banana that likes to dance?

A: **A banana shake!**

Q: Why did the boy bring a ladder to school?

A: **He wanted to go to high school!**

Q: Why did the spider go on the internet?

A: **To make a Webpage!**

Q: What is red and goes up and down?

A: **A tomato in an elevator!**

Q: What did the banana in the sun say to the other banana in the sun?
A: **I'm starting to peel!**

Q: Why did Phillip think he was built upside down?
A: **Because his feet smelt and his nose ran!**

Q: If you had 5 oranges in one hand and 5 pears in the other hand what would you have?

A: Massive hands!

Q: Why was 6 afraid of 7?

A: Because 7 ate 9!

Q: What do elves learn in school?

A: The elf-abet!

Q: How do you make a tissue dance?

A: You put a little boogie in it!

Q: What is a ghost's favorite dessert?

A: I-scream!

Q: What kind of mistake does a ghost make?

A: A boo-boo!

Q: Where do baby ghosts go during the day?

A: Day-scare centers!

Q: Where do ghosts mail their letters?
A: At the ghost office!

Q: What did the polite ghost say to her son?
A: Don't spook until your spooken to!

Q: Why did the boy have his girlfriend put in jail?
A: She stole his heart!

Q: What happens if you eat yeast and shoe polish?
A: Every morning you'll rise and shine!

Q: What did one volcano say to the other?

A: I lava you.

Q: What did the octopus say to his girlfriend when he proposed?

A: Can I have your hand, hand, hand, hand, hand, hand, hand, hand in marriage?

Q: What do ghosts eat for dinner?
A: Spook-eti!

Q: What do you do when 50 zombies surround your house?
A: Hope it is Halloween!!

Q: What is the most important subject a witch learns in school?
A: Spelling!

Q: Why didn't the skeleton want to go to school?
A: His heart wasn't in it.

Q: Why did the skeleton cross the road?
A: To get to the body shop.

Q: Why didn't the skeleton go to the ball?
A: Because he had no BODY to go with!
Q: Why are ghosts so bad at lying?
A: Because you can see right through them!

Q: Who did Frankenstein take to the dance?
A: His "ghoul" friend!

Q: What do ghosts use to wash their hair?
A: Sham-boo!

Frankenstein: Witch can you make me lemonade?
Witch: Poff! You are lemonade!

Q: What do you get when you cross a witch with sand?
A: A sandwich!

Q: Why is a skeleton so mean?
A: He doesn't have a heart!

*"Mommy, everyone says I look like a
werewolf."*
"Please be quiet and comb your face."

Q: Why do ghosts make good cheerleaders?
A: **Because they have a lot of spirit.**

Q: What did one owl say to the other owl?
A: **Happy Owl-ween!**

Q: What did the ghost say to the other ghost?

A: **Do you believe in humans?**

Q: Why do Mummies like the holidays?

A: **Because of all the wrapping!**

Q: Why does everybody like a Snowman?

A: **Because he is so cool!**

Q: Which letter of the alphabet has the most water?

A: **The letter C.**

Q: What do you call a skeleton that rests all day?

A: Lazy bones!

Q: What did the boy ghost ask the girl ghost?

A: Will you be my ghoul-friend?

Q: What happened when the young witch misbehaved?

A: She was sent to her broom!

Q: What is a ghost's favourite position playing soccer?

A: Ghoul keeper!

Q: Why don't witches ride their brooms
when they are angry?

A: They are afraid of flying off the handle!

Q: What makes a skeleton laugh?

A: When someone tickles his funny bone!

Q: What do goblins mail to friends from their holidays?
A: Ghost-cards!

Q: Why did the golfer wear two pairs of pants?
A: In case he got a hole in one!

Q: What race is never run?
A: A swimming race!

It's been scientifically proven that too many birthdays can kill you!

Q: What did one flea say to the other?
A: Should we walk or take a dog?

Q: Why do dogs run in circles?
A: Because it is hard to run in squares!

Q: Why don't dogs make good dancers?
A: Because they have two left feet!

Q: Why doesn't the elephant use a computer?

A: Because it is afraid of the mouse!

Q: What time is it when an elephant sits on the fence?

A: Time to fix the fence!

Q: How does an elephant put his trunk in a crocodile's mouth?

A: VERY carefully!

Q: What room does a ghost not need?

A: A living room!

Doctor, Doctor, Doctor, You've got to help me - I just can't stop my hands shaking.
Do you drink a lot?
Not really - I spill most of it!

Doctor, Doctor, Doctor, I've got wind! Can you give me something?
Yes - here's a kite!

Doctor, Doctor, Doctor, everyone keeps throwing me in the garbage.
Don't talk rubbish!

Doctor, Doctor, Doctor, I feel like a pack of cards.
I'll deal with you later.

Doctor, Doctor, Doctor, everyone thinks I'm a liar.
I don't believe that!

Doctor, Doctor, Doctor, when I press with my finger here... it hurts, and here... it hurts, and here... and here... What do you think is wrong with me?
You have a broken finger!

Doctor, Doctor, Doctor, I snore so loud I keep myself awake.

Sleep in another room then!

Doctor, Doctor, Doctor, I'm becoming invisible.

Yes I can see you're not all there!

Doctor, Doctor, Doctor, everyone keeps ignoring me.

Next please!

Doctor, Doctor, Doctor, I keep thinking I'm a dog.

Sit on the couch and we will talk about it.

But I'm not allowed up on the couch!

Doctor, Doctor, Doctor, I've lost my memory!
When did this happen?
When did <u>what</u> happen?

Doctor, Doctor, Doctor, I keep seeing double.
Please sit on the couch.
Which one!?

Doctor, Doctor, Doctor, I keep seeing an
insect spinning around.
*Don't worry; it is just a bug that's going
around!*

Doctor, Doctor, Doctor, I feel like a needle.
I see your point!

Doctor, Doctor, Doctor, what did the x-ray of
my head show?
Absolutely nothing!

Doctor, Doctor, Doctor, I'm a burglar!
Have you taken anything for it?

Doctor, Doctor, Doctor, I feel like an apple.
We must get to the core of this!

Q: Why don't eggs tell jokes?
A: Because they would crack each other up!

Q: Why was the maths book sad?
A: Because it had too many problems!

Q: What's the king of the pencil case?
A: The ruler!

Q: Have you heard about the mathematical plant?

A: It has square roots!

Q: Which tables do you not have to learn?

A: Dinner tables!

Q: What is 8.65 x 41 +8.6/72 x 945?

A: A headache!

Q: How do you make one vanish?

A: Add a 'g' to the beginning and it's gone!

Q: How do you make a witch itch?
A: Take away her W!

Q: What do witches race on?
A: Vroom-sticks!

Q: What is the problem with twin witches?
A: You never know which witch is which!

Q: What do you call two witches sharing an apartment?
A: Broom-mates!

Q: What does it mean if you find a horseshoe?

A: Some poor horse is walking around in his socks.

Q: What is the difference between a horse and a duck?

A: One goes quick and the other goes quack!

Q: What's a horse's favourite sport?

A: Stable tennis!

Today I gave my dead batteries away....Free of charge.

Q: What do you call a horse that lives next door?

A: A neighhhhh-bour.

Q: Where do horses go when they're sick?

A: The horse-pital.

Q: There were four cats in a boat, one jumped out. How many were left?

A: None. They were all copy cats!

Q: What is a cat's favourite colour?

A: Purrr-ple!

Q: What kind of cats like to go bowling?
A: **Alley cats!**

Q: Why do cats make terrible story tellers?
A: **They only have one tail.**

Q: What's a crocodile's favourite game?
A: **Snap!**

Q: What stays in the corner and travels all over the world?
A: **A stamp!**

Q: What's small, furry and bright purple?
A: A koala holding its breath!

Q: Why do mother kangaroo dislike bad weather?
A: Their joeys have to play inside!

Q: How do you make seven an even number?
A: Take the s out!

Q: What do you do if your dog chews your dictionary?
A: Take the words out of his mouth!

Q: What do you call a thieving alligator?

A: A crook-odile!

Q: What goes tick-tock, bow-wow, tick-tock, bow-wow?

A: A watch dog!

Q: What do you call a cow that eats your grass?
A: A lawn moo-er!

Q: What do you call a girl with a frog on her head?
A: Lilly!

Q: How does a dog stop a video?
A: He presses the paws button!

Q: What is the snake's favorite subject?
A: Hiss-story!

Q: Why does a dog wag its tail?

A: Because no one else will wag it for him!

Q: How do you make a goldfish old?

A: Take away the g!

Q: Why did the lamb cross the road?

A: To get to the baaaaarber shop!

Q: How does a mouse feel after it takes a shower?

A: Squeaky clean!

Q: What has four legs and goes "Oom, Oom"?

A: A cow walking backwards!

Q: What does a cat say when somebody steps on its tail?

A: Me-OW!

Q: What do you call a baby bear with no teeth?

A: A gummy bear!

Q: What do you call a cow in a tornado?
A: A milkshake!

Q: What do you call a deer with no eyes?
A: No I deer!

Q: What do you call an exploding monkey?
A: A baboom!

Q: What do you call an elephant in a phone booth?
A: Stuck!

Q: What do you call a sleeping bull?
A: A bulldozer!

Q: How do you stop a dog barking in the back seat of a car?
A: Put him in the front seat!

Q: What is the difference between a car and a bull?
A: A car only has one horn!

Q: Why do cows wear bells?
A: Because their horns don't work!

Q: How do you get a dog to stop digging in the garden?
A: Take away his shovel!

Q: What did one cow say to the other?
A: Mooooooove over!

Q: What kind of cat should you never play games with?
A: A cheetah!

Q: What did the banana do when the monkey chased it?
A: The banana split!

Q: What do you call a gorilla wearing earmuffs?

A: Anything you like, he can't hear you!

Q: What is the easiest way to count a herd of cattle?

A: With a cow-culator!

Q: What do you get from a bad-tempered shark?

A: As far away as possible!

Customer: "Do you have alligator shoes?"
Store person: "Yes, sir. What size does your alligator wear?"

Q: What fish only swims at night?
A: Starfish!

Q: Why did the elephant leave the circus?
A: He was tired of working for peanuts!

Q: Why was the mouse afraid of the water?
A: Catfish!

Q: How many skunks does it take to make a big stink?

A: A phew!

Q: How do you keep a skunk from smelling?

A: Plug its nose!

Q: What do you call a 400-pound gorilla?

A: Sir!

Q: What do fish take to stay healthy?

A: Vitamin sea!

Q: What do you call a mad elephant?
A: **An earthquake!**

Q: Where do baby apes sleep?
A: **In apricots!**

Q: What time is it when an elephant sits on your bed?
A: **Time to get a new bed!**

Q: Where does a ten ton elephant sit?
A: Anywhere it wants to!

Q: Where are sharks from?
A: Finland!

Q: What does an octopus wear when it gets cold?
A: A coat of arms!

Q: What does a calf become after its 1 year old?
A: 2 years old!

Q: Why does a giraffe have such a long neck?
A: Because his feet stink!

Q: What's a dog's favorite food for breakfast?
A: Pooched eggs!

Q: What do you give a pig with a rash?
A: Oinkment!

Q: What do you do if your cat swallows your pencil?
A: Use a pen!

Q: What kind of mouse does not eat, drink, or even walk?

A: A computer mouse!

Q: Why did the dinosaur cross the road?

A: The chicken wasn't around yet!

Q: What do you call snake with no clothes on?

A: Ssss-naked!

Q: Where do cows go on Saturday night?

A: To the mooooooovies!

Q: What do you call a dinosaur that never gives up?

A: A try and try and try-ceratops!

Q: What has ears like a cat and a tail like a cat, but is not a cat?

A: A kitten!

Q: What's a puppy's favorite kind of pizza?

A: Pup-peroni!

Q: What do camels use to hide themselves?

A: Camel-flauge!

Q: What did the porcupine say to the cactus?
A: Is that you Mummy?

Q: What is a frog's favorite year?
A: A leap Year!

Q: Why do pandas like old movies?
A: Because they are black and white!

Q: How many sheep do you need to make a sweater?
A: I don't know. I didn't think sheep could knit!

Q: What do you call a bruise on a T-Rex?
A: **A dino-sore!**

Q: When should you buy a bird?
A: **When it's going cheep!**

Q: Why did the little bird get in trouble at school?
A: **Because he was caught tweeting on a test!**

Q: What do you give a sick bird?
A: **Tweet-ment.**

Q: How do chickens get strong?
A: Egg-cersize.

Q: What robs you while you're in the bathtub?
A: A robber ducky.

Q: What do you call a sad bird?
A: A bluebird!

Q: What kind of math do Owls like?
A: Owl-gebra!

Q: What do you call a fish with no eye?
A: Fsh.

Q: Why wouldn't they let the butterfly into the dance?
A: Because it was a mothball!

Q: Who comes to a picnic but is never invited?
A: Ants!

Q: What letter can hurt you if it gets too close?

A: Bee!

Q: Why are A's like flowers?

A: Because bee's come after them!

Q: What is on the ground and also a hundred feet in the air?

A: A centipede on its back!

Q: What do frogs order when they go to a restaurant?

A: French Flies!

Q: What do you call a fly without wings?

A: A walk.

Q: Why was the ant so confused?

A: Because all his uncles were "ants"!

I tried to catch some fog earlier. I mist.

Q: What goes 99 thump, 99 thump, 99 thump?

A: A centipede with a wooden leg!

Q: What's worse than a worm in your apple?

A: Half a worm!

Q: What do you get when you cross a ghost and a cat?

A: A scaredy cat!

Q: What do you get when you cross a fish with an elephant?

A: Swimming trunks!

Q: What do you get when you cross a lemon and a cat?

A: A sourpuss!

Q: What do you get when you cross a fly, a car, and a dog?

A: A flying car-pet!

Q: What do you get if you cross a kangaroo and a snake?

A: A jump rope!

Q: What do you get when you cross an elephant with a witch?

A: I don't know but she will need a very large broom!

Q: What do you get if you cross a kangaroo and an elephant?

A: **Big holes all over Australia!**

Q: What do you get when you cross a porcupine and a turtle?

A: **A slowpoke!**

Q: Why did the sun go to school?
A: To get brighter!

Q: How do you know when the moon has enough to eat?
A: When it's full!

Q: Why don't monsters eat clowns?
A: Because they taste funny!

Q: What is an astronaut's favorite key on the keyboard?
A: The space bar!

Q: What did the alien say to the cat?
A: Take me to your litter!

Q: What do you call a crazy spaceman?
A: An astro-nut!

Q: Why did the people not like the restaurant on the moon?
A: Because there was no atmosphere!

Q: Who says sticks and stones may break my bones, but words will never hurt me?

A: A guy who has never been hit with a dictionary!

Q: How do you make a fire with two sticks?

A: Make sure one is a match!

Q: Why can't you say a joke while standing on ice?

A: Because it might crack up!

Q: What is at the end of everything?

A: The letter G!

Q: What nails do carpenters hate to hit?
A: Fingernails!

Q: How do locomotives hear?
A: Through the engineers!

Q: Why is tennis such a loud game?
A: Because each player raises a racquet!

Q: What two things can you not have for breakfast?
A: Lunch and dinner!

Q: Why did the belt go to jail?
A: It held up a pair of pants!

Q: What did the light bulb say to its mother?
A: **I wuv you watts and watts!**

Q: How can you tell that a train just went by?
A: **It left its tracks!**

Q: Why is it not safe to sleep on trains?
A: **Because they run over sleepers!**

Q: Have you heard the joke about the butter?
A: **I better not tell you, it might spread!**

Q: Why was the mushroom invited to lots of parties?

A: Because he was a fungi to be with!

Q: What's the tallest building in the world?

A: The library, because it has the most stories!

Q: Where are cars most likely to get flat tires?

A: At the forks in the road!

Q: Why was the calendar worried?

A: Its days were numbered!

Q: What school do you have to drop out of to graduate from?

A: Parachute school!

Q: What kind of phones do people in jail use?

A: Cell phones!

Q: What kind of driver has no arms or legs?
A: A screwdriver!

Q: Which runs faster, hot or cold water?
A: Hot, because you can catch cold!

Q: How does the ocean say hello?
A: It waves!

Q: What kind of underwear do reporters wear?
A: News briefs.

Q: What did one wall say to the other?
A: I'll meet you at the corner!

Q: Why does a flamingo lift up one leg?
A: Because if it lifted up both legs it would fall over!

Q: Why didn't the girl take the bus home?
A: Because her parents would make her take it back!

Q: What is the difference between a locomotive engineer and a teacher?
A: One minds the train, one trains the mind!

Q: Why did the thief take a shower?
A: He wanted to make a clean getaway!

Q: What does one bucket say to the other?
A: I am feeling pale today!

Q: Once there was a family called the Biggers. There was Mr. Bigger, Mrs. Bigger, and their son. Who was the biggest?
A: The son, because he was a little Bigger!

Q: What is worse than having one baby screaming?

A: Two babies screaming!

Q: Why did the boy take a ruler to bed?

A: To see how long he slept!

Q: Why did the melon jump into the lake?

A: It wanted to be a watermelon!

Q: Why was the boy sitting on his watch?

A: Because he wanted to be on time!

Q: Why can't a bicycle stand up?

A: Because it's two tired!

Q: What did one tooth say to the other tooth?

A: The dentist is taking me out tonight!

Q: How did the butcher introduce his wife?

A: Meet Patty!

Q: What did the lawyer name his daughter?

A: Sue!

Q: What did the calculator say to the math student?

A: You can count on me!

Q: What did the teddy bear say when it was offered dessert?

A: No thank you, I'm stuffed!

Q: Why was the woman fired from the car assembly line?

A: She was caught taking a brake!

Q: Why are kindergarten teachers so good?
A: They make the little things count!

Q: What letter can you drink?
A: T!

Q: What happened when the monster ate the electric company?
A: It was in shock for a week!

Q: When is a car not a car?
A: When it turns into a garage!

Q: Why did the tree go to the dentist?
A: It needed a root canal!

Q: What is always hot in the refrigerator?
A: Chilli!

Q: What did one flower say to the other flower?
A: Hey, bud!

Q: Why was the vacationing doctor so mad?
A: He had no patients!

Q: How do you cut a wave in half?
A: Use a sea saw!

Q: If you drop a white hat into the Red Sea, what does it become?
A: Wet!

Q: What kind of dress can't be worn?
A: Address!

Q: What has legs but doesn't walk?
A: A bed!

Q: What kinds of balls do dragons play soccer with?
A: Fireballs!

Q: Where do all the letters sleep?
A: In the alpha-bed!

Q: What has a bed that you can't sleep in?
A: A river!

Q: What is only a small box but can weigh
over a hundred pounds?
A: A scale!

Q: Where do computers go to dance?
A: The disk-o!

Q: When is a door not a door?
A: **When it's a-jar!**

Q: Where do soldiers keep their armies?
A: **In their sleeves!**

Q: Why don't honest people need beds?
A: **They don't lie!**

Q: How are doughnuts and golf alike?
A: **They both have a hole in one!**

Q: Why did the drum take a nap?

A: It was beat!

Q: What kind of band can't play music?

A: A rubber band!

Q: What room can you not go into?
A: **A mushroom!**

Q: What did the candle say to the other candle?
A: **I'm going out tonight!**

Q: Why did a boy throw a clock out the window?
A: To see time fly!

Q: Why did the girl throw the butter out the window?
A: She wanted to see a butterfly!

Q: What has four legs but never stands?
A: A Chair!

Q: What did the clock do after it ate?
A: It went back four seconds!

Q: What goes up and down but never moves?
A: Stairs!

Q: Why should you never tell a secret in a corn field?
A: Because there are too many ears!

Q: What goes on and on and has an 'i' in the middle?
A: An onion!

Q: Where does a boat go when it is sick?
A: To the dock!

Doctor, Doctor, Doctor, I keep getting pains in the eye when I drink coffee.
Have you tried taking the spoon out?

Doctor, Doctor, Doctor, I think I need glasses.
Yes you do, Sir, this is a butchers!

Doctor, Doctor, Doctor, I think I'm suffering from Deja Vu!
Didn't I see you yesterday?

Doctor, Doctor, Doctor, I feel like a sheep.
That's baaaaaaaaaad!

Doctor, Doctor, Doctor, I keep thinking I'm a mosquito.
Go away, sucker!

Doctor, Doctor, Doctor, Have you got something for a bad headache?
Yes.   Just take this hammer and hit yourself in the head. Then you'll have a bad headache.

Doctor, Doctor, Doctor, Can I have second opinion?
Of course, come back tomorrow!

Doctor, Doctor, Doctor, you have to help me out!
Certainly, which way did you come in?

Doctor, Doctor, Doctor, I keep thinking I'm invisible.
Who said that?

Q: What are prehistoric monsters called when they sleep?
A: A dino-snores!

Q: How many balls of string would it take to reach the moon?
A: Just one if it's long enough!

Q: What do elves do after school?
A: Gnomework!

Q: What is heavier, a full moon or a half moon?
A: The full moon because it's lighter!

Q: What is the best hand to write with?
A: Neither - it's best to write with a pen!

Q: Why is a horse like a wedding?
A: Because they both need a GROOM!!!

Q: Did you hear the joke about the pencil?
A: But it doesn't have any point!

Q: Why do nutters eat biscuits?
A: Because they're crackers!

Q: Who invented fire?
A: Some bright spark!

Q: Why do birds fly south in the winter?
A: Because it's too far to walk!

Q: What is "out of bounds"?
A: An exhausted kangaroo!

Q: Where does success come before work?
A: In the dictionary!

Q: What is the strongest bird?
A: A crane!

Q: Where do snowmen go to dance?
A: A snowball!

Q: What kind of fish can't swim?
A: Dead ones!

Q: How do you make milk shake?
A: Give it a good scare!

Q: Do you know the time?
A: No, we haven't met yet!

Q: What lies at the bottom of the sea and shivers?
A: A nervous wreck!

Q: What sort of animal is a slug?
A: A snail with a housing problem!

Q: What is a "Minimum" mean?
A: A very small mother!

Q: What does "Maximum" mean?
A: A very big mother!

Q: What holds the sun up in the sky?
A: Sunbeams!

Q: Why did cavemen draw pictures of hippopotamuses and rhinoceroses on their walls?
A: Because they couldn't spell their names!

Can I have a hair-cut please?
Certainly, which one!?

Q: What kind of bee drops things?
A: **Fumble bee!**

Q: What did the bee say to the flower?
A: Hello honey!

Q: What did the confused bee say?
A: To bee or not to bee!

Q: What are the cleverest bees?
A: Spelling bees!

The End